THE MENTAL INERTIA

A Look into How Our Brains Work Similar to the Laws of Physics

ADITYA BIKRAM SINGH

Copyright © Aditya Bikram Singh 2024
All Rights Reserved.

ISBN 979-8-89233-367-2

This book has been published with all efforts taken to make the material error-free after the consent of the author. However, the author and the publisher do not assume and hereby disclaim any liability to any party for any loss, damage, or disruption caused by errors or omissions, whether such errors or omissions result from negligence, accident, or any other cause.

While every effort has been made to avoid any mistake or omission, this publication is being sold on the condition and understanding that neither the author nor the publishers or printers would be liable in any manner to any person by reason of any mistake or omission in this publication or for any action taken or omitted to be taken or advice rendered or accepted on the basis of this work. For any defect in printing or binding the publishers will be liable only to replace the defective copy by another copy of this work then available.

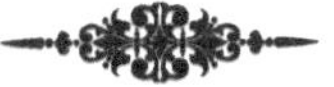

Dedication

To my parents, my pillars of strength.

Whatever dreams, achievements, and efforts that are borne out of me are a projection of them

My entire being is for their service and happiness.

Contents

Preface

The idea to conceive this book occurred to me amidst the toughest exam I had ever encountered—my final year MBBS exams. Reflecting on my journey since NEET preparation times, where I overcame obstacles and constant failures, faced disappointments, and rebounded to start from scratch to conquer the last lap—I wish to share a small piece of my struggles with everyone who might be in need of some help.

Some of the ideas are completely my own, while others draw inspiration from a myriad of sources—the dead, the living, the artificial, and the imaginary.

Chapter 1

Inertia

At the beginning of any huge task, you find yourself surrounded by so much uncertainty.

This uncertainty gives birth to a fear that gets embedded so deep into you that you are afraid to even take the first step. You want to pretend it isn't real, it isn't near, or that it cannot possibly do much harm if you start it a little late. Your subconsciousness pumps up so many excuses that you finally convince your mind that it is too much effort to start. You get defeated even before starting your quest and believe that it is the best for you.

You are wrong.

The only thing inevitable is a pang of regret. Ages later, when you have lost your energy and youth, and all doors of opportunities are closed, you will regret that you should have taken that chance and gone for it. Because you will be once again far from reality and can imagine whatever you want for your past, you will always end up in regret, whether you want to truly believe it or not.

Unless you are comfortable with how your life is going or want to remain mediocre forever.

This **hesitation** to start new things or to continue an old abandoned project, is something that all of us face. It is inevitable. It is in our very nature. We are beings wired for survival and do not want to start a venture unless success is guaranteed with 100% certainty. If there's at least one commonality between you and Elon Musk or Mark Zuckerberg, or take any hot shot young entrepreneur, it is this—they too faced this resistance. The difference? You already know it.

Let us talk about two things regarding the dynamics of resistance—inertia and momentum.

Our minds operate much like real-life objects. They follow the laws of physics, or the laws of motion to be more specific. If you've studied science till at least 10th grade then you already know what I'm talking about. If not, or if you want to refresh your memory, here is a little recapitulation.

- The first law of motion:

An object at rest will remain at rest or an object in motion will remain so unless an external force acts on it.

Now, applying this law in real life—If you are in a state of dormancy, lying in bed all day, doing nothing, procrastinating things to kingdom come, you will remain as such. This is **inertia.**

Whereas if you are on a streak of doing things, setting deadlines, completing your objectives, winning achievements, and getting your tasks done; you won't have much difficulty in continuing to do so. This is **momentum.**

The mind thinks with what it currently has. If you are stacking up wins, you are afraid to lose and so you continue to work harder and harder. Your wins will become greater and the pressure to keep it together will keep pushing you to the very limits of your abilities. This is what 'living on the edge' feels like. Whereas, if you do nothing, there won't be pressure to do anything. Even the slightest bit of effort will seem like a huge burden! I remember, once, when I had bunked classes for a couple of days and was just lazing around in my room, I felt thirsty. I was on my bed and the bottle was only a couple of metres away on a table. I was about to go to sleep but I decided that I'd rather wake up with dehydration than get up, walk to the bottle, and drink water! Yes! And I'm writing this book with such big talk! I know.

We all vary in our levels of inertia. That's the reason you see there is so much diversity in the results and productivity of people around you. People with low inertia can do anything quickly and at a moment's notice. They feel energetic most of the time and it could be said that they are mostly extroverts. However, they may be easily distracted or lose their will to work even with the slightest bit of resistance. They are the ones who come up with freaky ideas and innovative ventures but are the first ones to bail out once things stop going their way.

People with high inertia, on the other hand, are the ones who procrastinate more often. They'll put off work till the very last moment possible, seek help from others if it's available, are masters of copy-pasting, and usually spend 90% of their time binge-watching a show, reading comics, or playing games. They are mostly introverts, keeping to themselves and enjoying their own company. But, once they set their mind to doing something, they will keep pouring their life energy into it until they achieve what they want. They tend to be far less distracted than people with low inertia.

Which one is better? There is no one-size-fits-all answer to that. The answers are circumstantial.

People with high inertia might find themselves in a difficult situation to pursue everyday jobs. They get tired very easily, easily losing motivation to go to work every day for a living. However, give them a single project and task and they will surprise you with their energy because following that one task, a sense of freedom opens up for them to relish. People with low inertia, on the other hand, might be good at managerial work. They do not find difficulty in switching tasks and managing multiple tasks at once. Even if they get tired, just a little motivation will lift their spirits and they will be back to work.

The introverts and extroverts being people with high and low inertia are just mere personal speculation. It doesn't matter what you are because the dynamic states of inertia and momentum are interlinked with two other factors which are the variables for the different types of situations we face. They are **resistance** and the **driving force.**

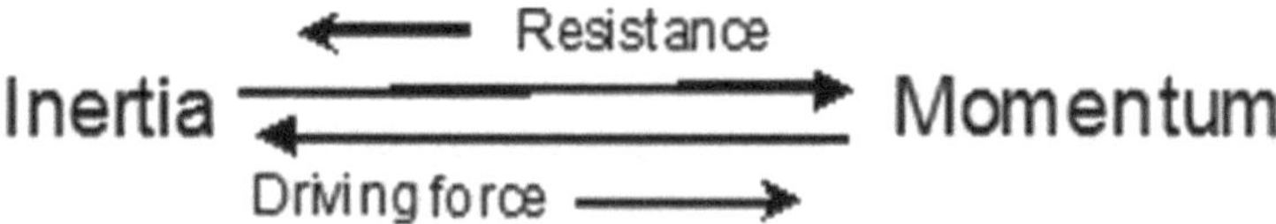

Chapter 2

Resistance and Momentum

So what is this resistance that prevents us from doing our work?

Resistance is the innate force that wants to keep things as they are. It is a **force that resists change.** A force that increases the inertia of rest of a person.

In physics, it can be compared to friction.

As we know, friction is a self-limiting force. This means that it is a force that automatically adjusts itself according to the counterforce applied. In simple words, the harder the goal you set, the greater the resistance that you are going to face.

Resistance can be categorised into **internal resistance** and **external resistance**. You don't need a master's degree in science to figure out what they are, but I'm going to say it anyway.

Internal resistance is composed of your primal fears, your personality, your past trauma, and the burden of your past mistakes all summed up into one giant monster that pulls you from moving forward. External resistance, though not as big as the internal one, is composed of the circumstances surrounding your work. Your toxic boss or teammates, the shitty dorm that you live in, lack of money, lack of a proper platform to begin from— the list is endless. Both kinds of resistances are huge right in the beginning but they lose power as you start to move.

Resistance, no matter how evil it may seem, also serves as a kind of pathfinder. You will know that you are going in the right direction only if you encounter resistance— the right amount of it. Too much resistance would mean you are unskilled for pursuing your current aspiration, so go back and prepare again. Whereas, too little resistance would indicate that you might be using unfair means or you are being duped.

There comes a point in everyone's lives, where even after starting correctly and seemingly defeating this monster of resistance, we encounter such a huge roadblock that we lose all our will to continue. We will talk more about this in Chapter 10.

Steven Pressfield has beautifully outlined the concept of resistance in his book titled *Do the Work*. It is a great book that I recommend reading if you want to know more about how resistance works. If not, you are already overpowered by resistance.

Just kidding. This is what you need to know—Resistance is your own shadow. It will never leave your side. It will grow as you grow.

Now let's talk about momentum. Recall the moment when your shift was about to end, but you noticed a minor but critical correction that needed to be done. Despite being exhausted you still wanted to finish it off before leaving because you didn't want to keep things for later. The reason for this is simple. It is much easier to finish tasks while you are already working rather than beginning them after a long break. This phenomenon happens because you are in a state of inertia of motion.

Since you are already in motion (doing tasks) you will continue to do work without getting affected.

Momentum is what you gain while working. Reach enough momentum and you reach a state where you feel unstoppable. You get things done easily. You know your way out of the obstacles and dead ends. You have a clear picture in your mind of what you want to achieve and you can see yourself progressing towards it. This momentum will eventually propel you to a state called **'The Zone'** where you feel like you are invincible. I have talked in detail about this in Chapter 9.

To sum it up, you know and enjoy what you want to do. When you are in momentum, you are in a state of maximum work efficiency. Your employers, if any would be proud of you in this state. So when we are working, studying, or pursuing any creative activity, we must strive to achieve momentum as fast as possible and to reduce resistance (more so, our internal forces) as much as possible.

The last component of the inertia-momentum complex is the **driving force**. It is the sum total of all the factors in your life that drive you towards your goal. The depth of your aspirations, the necessity and circumstances that make you choose your career path, and the promises made to your close ones—these form the major chunk of the driving force. It is permanent in nature but it is imbued in your subconscious and does not provide much fuel to your momentum. But you can count on it to continually propel you forward through hardships and difficulties.

On the other hand, the tiny forces of encouragement that you get from your peers and family, the motivation that you draw from your guides, and the inspiration that you seek from your idols, are temporary but provide huge bursts of energy to do short tasks. They are, however, transient and will lose effect after a while, until you find a new source of motivation.

Like everything in nature, all forces must be balanced to be sustainable. So is the case with this complex. We must understand that resistance is a necessary evil. Without resistance, people will be lost and helpless. They won't have the drive to work and produce new things. The satisfaction at the end of a job won't be there. They will just be like robots doing mundane tasks.

So when you find that you are not finding enough resistance while doing a job, take it as a cue that it is time to raise your threshold. The time has come to upgrade yourself, enhance your skills, and be a better version of yourself to work more, suffer more, endure more, and keep moving forward. Otherwise, you will just stay where you are, become stagnant, and slowly rot into mediocrity.

Chapter 3

The Power of Work

If you're an Indian kid, you would have certainly heard the incessant praise showered upon the class topper. The *'Sharmaji ka beta'*; the all-knowing, ever-punctual, perfectionist whose mere existence is a bane to your survival in your house; The guy who does everything so well, every parent wants to adopt that kid as their own.

You hear all kinds of things about him—he's gifted, he's talented, he's God's favourite child, and similar phrases. And after some time, you just get irritated whenever that kid's name is uttered. Sometimes, you end up wishing to do something totally different than what he did just to get rid of the comparison. Or sometimes, you accept your failure and remain so, hoping that your parents will stop praising him so much.

What Indian parents do not understand is that their child gets hurt with each passing praise, for you're comparing your child with that guy subconsciously. What will a child think? When he constantly hears that someone is so good, he is bound to feel that he must be lagging behind. Too much of it and he just accepts his state. They are not promoting any kind of healthy competition here by bringing out that someone is better than their child. Rather focusing on their own child will ensure that he has a good and lovable childhood. They don't realise that their child can be scared to take decisions for himself, have his favourites, or even choose something for himself when he's out with his friends.

No, I am not haunted by my past and am not talking about myself. Do not assume that. You are wrong. Absolutely wrong.

Enough talk about our parents. Let's come back to what we can control. So, all this praising of others' kids must certainly be bringing your motivation down. Your driving force is severely affected by this. One ends up thinking,

What's the point of studying further anyway? I'm not talented. What's the point of even working hard?

So in this chapter, I'm going to tell you what power you possess that a talented child lacks—

The ability to infinitely work hard without fear of failure.

Child prodigies rarely make it big later in their lives. It is for the simple reason that they are showered with so much love and affection from the beginning that they eventually forget how much hard work it requires later. When they are confronted with reality, it is too hard for them to accept it and they just give in. I have had a friend who used to be the class topper right from the beginning. My entire childhood, I was taunted by his name. But now, he is the only one who is still penniless while the rest have started earning. He is still preparing for entrance exams while his peers have passed out and joined residency.

I'll tell you about two people—both cousins. One who is a very popular biologist forever immortalised in the textbooks of biology with his theory of evolution, Sir

Charles Darwin. And the other, who like many, faded in mediocrity, Sir Francis Galton.

Amongst both, who do you think was more 'gifted', more talented, and more suitable to inherit the family riches?

It was actually Galton.

Galton showed great aptitude for learning. He had the markings of a prodigy—a child genius. Yet, wanton destiny chose the man who persevered through the toils of hard work rather than the gifted man.

And Galton is not the only example. There are countless others—Johann Wolfgang Beethoven, Steve Jobs, Oprah Winfrey, and Thomas Edison to name a few.

So what is this thing that genius people tend to do that makes them falter and lose out on glory? This is an important question for you if you consider yourselves as one of the geniuses.

It is the tendency to be lazy and skip things for tomorrow.

They think they are so smart that they can always do their work in less time. Or, they need fewer revisions to study a subject. Or they don't even need to study something this early from the teacher. They can always learn it later.

This fatal mistake costs them in the long run. The inertia of winning may carry their winning streak ahead for some time, but the eventual outcome is already known. Any skill without practice becomes stale. The untalented guy knows that he doesn't have a knack for the subject or skill. Therefore, he goes the extra mile to know the nuances of it. He works hard and keeps working hard. He doesn't stop, for he knows that if he stops working hard, he will be thrown out of the competition in an instant. There is a necessity of working hard which keeps his driving force in peak form. This gradually increases his inertia from being a failure to keep winning every time. When the time comes to perform, the hardworking guy excels and fares much better than the talented guy.

There are also many well-known stories about people who stopped working hard once they reached a certain stardom and then their career had a dip. Sushil Kumar from *Kaun Banega Crorepati* is a prime example of this. The wealth he had won was wasted away in a matter of few years. Pride and greed are natural vices that grow when a person becomes successful. To keep them in check and to be humble till the last day of your work is the real test of a man.

The lesson is: Stay humble while you are practising or learning. *Karma* hates one thing and that is pride. So lower your head and keep doing your work till it is complete. You can boast all you want after your work is done. Let your work speak for itself.

Chapter 4

Smart Work: The Myth

You have likely come across the proverbial advice time and again, "Don't work hard, work smart." Then people go on to describe how a daily-wage labourer works so hard and yet gets a meagre salary while a businessman sitting in an office all day, doing practically no physical work, earns much more in comparison.

This is such a flawed comparison.

And this comparison is levied to many other professions. I see people comparing the work of a radiologist with that of a physician or a surgeon. Software engineers are compared with other professions. To all these comparisons, I just have one thing to say—the grass always looks greener on the other side.

It is in human nature to find flaws even in the most luxurious of lifestyles. Such is the human mind, a product of our evolutionary journey. We just cannot accept our successes, rather we have to find something that is troubling us in order to make sure that our posterity is secure. This urge to find flaws is permanent. Even if we become Gods, we cannot escape this urge. And thus, we bring down all the insecurity, sleepless nights, and anxiety upon ourselves. The mental exertion undertaken by a businessman surpasses that of a daily labourer. The businessman deals with managing, planning, predicting, accounting, and so much more. Sometimes, they also work overtime to fulfil their employer's quota.

Whereas the daily-wage labourer comes to work, does his designated job for a fixed amount of time, and then leaves. His work might have many more hazards than a businessman's, but is the measuring scale comparing both jobs accurate? I feel, for the same amount of money, the businessman or any skilled professional works much harder than the labourer.

This phrase, "Smart work over hard work", is catchy and appealing. It is highly infectious. Why? It appeals to you so much because it tends to make you lazy, shunning the hard part of working. People generally want to be regarded as geniuses rather than hard workers—the ones who get more done in less time. Because you have used your ingenious brain to cut short a huge load of burden that you had to endure, and reach your goal fast. So this adage is lucrative because it forces you to look for shorter and quicker alternatives than the usual way.

However, this adage is only for those who have had a considerable amount of experience in their work. So before all else, you must first put in the work. Work the traditional way. Find out the difficulties in your path, and only then try to look for alternatives.

In my case, I have seen people on YouTube giving advices like, "Don't waste your time making notes; do this and that fancy stuff which will help you save time, and do more in less time." This is the worst piece of advice that one can give to a beginner. A large number of people watching these videos will be beginners who are struggling to move out of their state of inertia. Watching these videos will make them think that by following these methods they can get away by working less. Believe me, I have tried all that and have failed miserably.

You will neither get your work done nor have the advantage of time that you had in the first place. You will end up wasting your time in a research frenzy searching for alternative methods, having already wasted a sizeable chunk of your time trying out the previous methods and failing, when the deadline is near. Just work the conventional way till you are tired and bored of it; Only then, set out to find something new.

Most people that you find exhibit high inertia. They will tend to procrastinate till the last minute, wasting time researching how to do things quickly rather than actually doing the work. This is why it is easy to differentiate yourself from the competition if you just stick to working hard consistently.

These days, the term 'hard work' is just frowned upon. But hard work isn't that hard at all! It is just work that needs to be done with a little investment of your time. It is the bare minimum and there is no other substitute for it.

Do not shun hard work. Take a comparison between any standard athlete and a person who is preparing for a national entrance test. The athlete starts training at a very young age. All her effort for an Olympic medal and training spanning a decade culminates in a mere few seconds or minutes of performance. It is either the glory of a lifetime or fading away in mediocrity. Half of your entire life, for just a few minutes of performance. And they still go for it? The other guy has to keep studying, has multiple attempts for the test, and doesn't bother much if he doesn't get the top rank. He just wants to clear the exam. That's why the sportsmen deserve a lot of admiration for their goals and aspirations.

Coming back to our discussion on hard work; Once you've achieved this bare minimum amount of work, any other work that you do is yours for the taking. You can call it, 'extra', 'hard', or 'smart' work—it's up to you. And it is this extra amount of work that actually sets you apart from the competition and tremendously increases your chance of getting what you want.

So, in the end, the word 'smart work' that you hear is just the extra amount of work done, not cutting corners of your actual work.

Chapter 5

Potential Energy

You must have faced a situation where, you started a task, a project, or a new venture extremely motivated. The driving force is so overpowering that you feel you are going to create a masterpiece. You lay out all plans, tell all your friends about this new venture, gather all the necessary material required for the venture, and start.

The beginning is amazing. Everything goes according to your plan. You enjoy what you are doing. Help pours in from all directions. People appreciate what you are doing. Everything is going smoothly.

And then, suddenly, without any prior notice or any kind of foreboding, you hit a roadblock.

Something or the other does not work out according to your plan. You see unforeseen setbacks which overwhelm your capacity to fight back and you lose all motivation to complete your task.

And that's the end of an incomplete masterpiece. One which couldn't see the light of the world. One which was abandoned without being fully realised. Something great that could never see the dawn of light and never reached the masses it was meant for. This is a fairly common occurrence in those who follow creative pursuits—artists, filmmakers, bookwriters, and so on. Especially, the amateurs and the beginners. But so does it happen with people beginning a new project in the workplace or people preparing for exams. It happens once to every individual.

So what happened really? The most common answer will be: I lost my motivation to do it.

And how did it come to this? You had it all worked out in the beginning, but something came in the way and you just stopped working for it.

When we dream, we rarely take into account the roadblocks that we are going to face. And most certainly, even if we prepare ourselves, there is always going to be something uncertain, something totally unknown, that is going to come and wreck our dreams to smithereens. This is a part of the **resistance**.

There is no easy solution or ultimate cure to remove this resistance. But there is a habit that will help you keep on track till you reach the end of the line. The end might be different from what you had envisioned. It could be better or may differ from your expectations. You may or may not like what you get in the end but it will make sure that you reach there. That habit is the habit of discipline.

Each man and woman have different capacities for hard work. This intrinsic capacity, **the potential energy** of each individual is made up of two components: discipline and motivation. Even if one component is higher in the beginning, the other will slowly but certainly follow up and become significant eventually.

You have low motivation to start but you know how hard you have to work and you still do it anyway, you will eventually come to fall in love with your work. You have an extreme desire to do something but you don't know how and what to do, things will start falling into place once you start working on it and you will develop a routine for it yourself after a certain period of time.

Motivation and inspiration—these devices are just like the spark plug. Their work is to provide the required ignition to make the engine run. What really keeps the car moving is the fuel. And that fuel is discipline. If the fuel is empty, no amount of ignition is going to move the car.

Many books talk about cultivating the habit of discipline, becoming focused, and increasing this potential energy within you but we will not spend any further time discussing that. What I will say is this—Discipline is like a sapling. It grows with you. It isn't something you are born with. It is a plant that requires continuous nurturing. Its only enemy is complacency. Once you get complacent, your discipline dies, and then you have to start all over again, watering it slowly from the start once again. That is why it is so much harder to return to an incomplete project.

You get used to discipline with time. It is a process that moulds you and shapes you into a different person. A better person. And once you are accustomed to it, you will feel it is natural to follow your routine. It becomes your shadow. Once you've attained this stage—the culmination of discipline and perseverance, i.e. 'The Zone'—it is hard for external forces and resistances to throw you off track.

But no matter how disciplined you are, you will face pitfalls on the way. There will be forces strong enough to break your momentum and slow you down if not completely stop you in your tracks. This is inevitable.

This is where you just take a short break and reacquire motivation. To rekindle the spark that is missing in your life.

Motivation is all around you. And it might come to you in the most unexpected of circumstances. You might not find it when you are looking for it, but it will definitely find you some time or the other. You will capture it in little things and events when the things that occur will make sense to you and only you. But rather than waiting for motivation to find you, go seek your motivation yourself. Taking a walk outside, watching inspirational videos, reading books, and listening to stories of those who have trodden a similar path to you, will help you find your way. You will find your motivation for certain.

Do not waste too much time searching for motivation or over-motivating yourself. There are potential dangers that lurk when you just keep getting motivated and don't do any work. Your ego convinces you that you are a great person and could corrupt you into thinking that you can do whatever you want and whenever you want thus making you override the practicalities of life.

Our lives are a series of mountains and valleys and we are a ball travelling through it. When we are going downhill, indeed our speed is up but when we reach rock bottom and start to climb up, that is when the extra motivation comes in to help us to climb up the pitfalls. It is just a series of highs and lows until we finally make it. All of us will eventually make it, but alas many give up before realising the meaning of this journey. Motivation will help you climb the toughest of mountains but discipline will keep you walking for long distances. Keep walking till you find what you want in your life.

Chapter 6

Impulse: The First Step

The theory and preaching part is over. Now let's start with practical problems.

Individuals usually encounter namely two emotions as they prepare to embark on a new venture. One faction is excited like anything as we discussed at the beginning of the previous chapter. They are ready to face the storm, mow down all the obstacles on the way, chew away the competition, and emerge victorious. The other faction is at the opposite end. They are afraid and nervous. They are hesitant to even take the first step of the journey. While the previous chapter was for the first category, this chapter is for the second category.

The biggest obstacle that you'd face at this stage—the base of the mountain that you want to climb—is the fear of failure. Your entire life you were protected by your parents, seniors, teachers, and friends. You grew up in a protected environment, you took decisions that were the safest and which assured success. So, why now? Why would you take the plunge now? Will it be worth it? You have just grown your wings; Are you confident that you will certainly fly? What if you crash down and lose the ability to fly forever?

Such thoughts must be crossing your mind. A dream unrealised is the most beautiful thing in the world. You can shape it all you want according to your fantasies. No setbacks, no accidents. Just a perfect world in an imaginary realm where you are the king. You don't want to spoil it. *What if things don't go my way? What if I fail? What if it doesn't work out as I have planned?* This attachment to perfectionism keeps you from working on your dream altogether. We are so attached to our dreams that we would rather not work on them than see them spoiled.

You don't even take the first step because you know well that once you take it, you owe a responsibility towards it—responsibility for its progress and completion, and its deterioration and failure alike. As funny as we are, we always look for excuses and other people to blame. If something doesn't work out, people need a name to be put forth as a sacrifice—a receptacle of their anguish and wrath. But who would you blame for not being able to achieve your dreams? No one other than you right? And can you keep on living with that guilt for the rest of your life?

No!

So let's just skip it and keep it in our dreams only. Let's not work on it. Life will be much easier that way.

And then you will die just like any other random nameless person. With no footprint left behind on earth. No one to remember you in the subsequent generations.

What I want to tell you now is what I've already told you in the first chapter. You are in a huge state of inertia at that moment. And once you start moving, gather enough courage, and take the first step; things will become less and less difficult. (Static friction is less than dynamic friction.)

To elucidate, once you start working, you start expanding your knowledge. You open yourself to a number of opportunities that you never thought existed. Sure, you might hit a roadblock but that makes you wiser. You will know how to avoid that roadblock the next time it comes your way. That is why it is utterly important to just start, to take the first step and get the ball moving.

A warning that must be given at this stage—keep in mind the Dunning Kruger effect. We tend to take things lightly right after starting off believing that we have reached the end of the skillset. It is at this stage where we are very prone to make mistakes while thinking we know it all and therefore should be careful.

Now, if you're in the first category of people—the ones motivated and confident enough to start their journey without any fear in their minds, I have a few words of advice for you: calm down and analyse. I know how hard it feels when you hit a roadblock and fall. When things don't go according to your plan, you might even stop taking risks forever!

Your priority should be to **analyse yourself**—your weaknesses, your perspective, your experience, and your past traumas. This shall pull you out of the golden dream world that you were seeing with sparkly eyes and put you back in reality, a pragmatic state, where you can weigh the consequences of your actions that you are going to take.

Next, you must do a bit more research. A little, not too much, mind you. Or you shall be stuck in a fever of researching every nook and cranny of your work and never actually work. Ask your seniors, read about the experiences of those who came before you, read books, articles, blogs, and posts about the topic that you want.

Earlier, I advised against researching too much because it puts you in a continuous state of doing research only. The more you read about something, the more problems you will find and you'll want to know about every little problem associated with that field. Thus, you'd spend all your time just researching and not actually doing any field work.

Learn, as you work. Know the practical problems while working and become wiser on the go. The wisdom you acquire this way sticks to you longer and clearer than any other experience you get in any other way.

Whatever faction you belong to, find the right balance, step out of your comfort zone, and just begin. Set the ball rolling and you will see the magic happening around you and within you.

Chapter 7

Rituals

We have talked about how to begin, and now we shall discuss how to keep things moving.

After you start your journey, there will come a point where inevitably, you will face so much resistance that you'll want to quit. This will happen faster if you keep things monotonous and don't do anything to make the basic work that you do look interesting.

Rituals are a way to do just that. I am not talking about any kind of religious practices or divine incantations. I am just talking about habits and practices that are purely personal and would augment your driving forces.

I would first describe a few things to keep in mind and then narrate a few personal rituals, those performed by my friends which helped us stay sane during our final medical exams.

Things to keep in mind:

1. Your ritual must be your personal practice. It shouldn't be copied or inspired by anyone else. Or you will lose interest in it soon

2. It must be performed daily or it will lose its importance. Performing it frequently in a day also diminishes its value so I would recommend a maximum of three times a day

3. If it is associated with a personal memory it is more effective. Something that reminds you of your past days, your peak performance, or your absolute low. Something that will stimulate you to work harder

4. It must be an activity, not imagination. Your nerve endings must get stimulated to get into work mode when you perform that act. Sitting and imagining your success will put you in a dream-like state, increase your inertia, and defeat the purpose of this exercise altogether

5. It can be anything. No activity is too high or too low to be transformed into a ritual. It can be a simple activity of making your bed right after you wake up, sweeping the floor before you sit to study, or even playing a stimulating game of chess for five minutes. It is your decision

6. The rituals that you perform must be immediately followed by the main activity that you want to perform—your work. The more you delay, the more you lose the ritual's power that is poured into you

These are a few beneficial things to kick-start your journey. The more you work on your rituals the more experience you will gather in using them.

All this sounds a little superstitious, right? Even though I have talked about so much of science before? Well, when you are pushed to the limits, even the most practical of men are forced to find hope in inanimate things.

In the words of Michael Scott, "I am not superstitious, I am a little-stitious," which is a good thing.

Here are some personal experiences of the rituals that I performed before I sat down to study.

At the very beginning, I used to outline my study objectives. I have seen that objectifying my study helped me focus better and I got distracted far too less than in those sessions where I just sat down to study aimlessly.

Next, I used to sit down and scroll random articles on *DeepStash.* It is a good app that summarises ideas/blogs/articles/books into a few-minute-readable micro post. It helped me get my mind into a state of curiosity and after a fixed amount of time, I immediately switched to reading my academic books, and that state of mind carried on with my studies.

In between, when I used to lose focus, I used to take my diary and write about my reading performance so far. How many of my objectives I have completed, how much time I have left, what distractive and unproductive thoughts surfaced while I studied, and any other thing that I wished to do but postponed because of my study session. This served as a personal conversation with myself, made me serious when I was lagging, and calmed me down when I was getting hyperactive or reading at such a fast pace that I would forget what I was reading. It brought in a balance that is needed for steady studying sessions.

I used to work out twice a day to keep my brain in an active state. I have seen that on the days when I don't work out, I feel lethargic throughout the day. Working out helped me to focus well when I studied. Having a good physique and fewer sickness spells were just secondary prerequisites that it provided.

Rarely, when I ran out of juice, I used to listen to music to calm my nerves. While studying, I used to listen to Lo-fi or classical music, sometimes *bhajans* and *kirtans* because they do not distract your mind too much; you don't listen to their tunes or lyrics actively and can keep playing in the background while you work. I could never study with lyrically-rich songs playing in the background as my thoughts always wandered off to the meaning behind the lines. The same goes for songs that have great music. Then I'd wander off into a fantasy world where I'd be fighting off demons or creating a new world with that music in play. If my mind craved such music while I was studying and it didn't let me study enough, I used to take a five-minute break, go outside, sit down, and listen to that one song; Only then I'd come back and resume.

These are a few things that I observed my friends doing—They used to go out, drink tea, and immediately come back and sit down to study, without wasting too much time in transit. I have seen some carrying tea to their study desks too, sipping it constantly while studying. I have seen others go and talk with a specific group of friends before sitting down to study, while some listened to a particular song, or talked on the phone with someone. All these rituals are personal effects that helped them focus and get through.

These are not absolutely necessary, but they help you move more smoothly in your journey. You can find your own ritual by observing your own daily routine or you may devise it *de novo* for your benefit. Experiment with different activities, find the one that suits you the best, and stick to it till you complete your objective. Keep repeating your rituals whenever you sit down and repeat the same activity.

Chapter 8

Distractions and Entropy

The biggest resistance there ever will be is distraction. It is also, the most convenient of excuses to give when you have lost motivation. You will find thousands of videos, hundreds of books, and scores of podcasts that talk about how to deal with distractions. And yet, no one has ever come to a definitive aid or cure.

What is the origin of distractions though? How do they come to existence? I mean, it is you and your work, right? So from where does a third entity come into play?

It all comes down to the play of chemicals inside your brain. The most notorious of them is dopamine—the reward chemical. The brain releases dopamine to reward ourselves for getting something that is 'ensuring our survival'. This is the reason your brain picks up a chocolate rather than a meal of salad because chocolate has more calories in it which will ensure more energy and thus a higher chance of survival in the wild. We might have evolved from prehistoric times but our brain hasn't. It still gauges the activities that we do in terms of survival. The activities that ensure our survival in the long run are: having sex (ensuring the continuity of our species) or eating a lavish meal (more calories = longer duration of survival). Thus we feel so good after doing such activities.

In the current generation, however, this reward system is outdated. Addictions and cravings have come into play which severely increase our inertia. Addictions are the activities you do that constantly release dopamine. Gradually, we develop a reliance on them for our dopamine. If we suddenly stop getting that dopamine hit, we might suffer serious health problems. Alcohol dependence is one such thing where the sudden withdrawal of alcohol causes symptoms like tremors, nausea, hallucinations, and even seizures.

Another thing is that, in this era, we are habituated to being distracted. We cannot concentrate for more than five to ten minutes on anything. We tend to drift off and switch open our phones instead and start idly scrolling.

We are used to seeing something moving and absorbing passive information all the time. This is more of a bad habit than a problem. And the cure for this is consciously trying to realise that it is a bad source of dopamine release which I had talked about earlier and to keep away from it as much as possible while trying to develop a counter habit.

The only way to break a habit is to **create a counter habit** for it. You trade in a good habit in lieu of the bad habit that you had. You must already know that it takes at least 21 days to break or make a habit and 90 days to integrate it into your lifestyle. So challenge yourself to stay away from your most distracting activities for 21 days and see the results for yourself.

When I was a kid, I used to play a lot of video games. There was one principle behind every game that I ever played. If you find enemies in your path, you're going in the right direction. Distractions are just like that. You won't ever be distracted when you're doing anything other than your actual work or when you're enjoying yourself. It will be ridiculous to hear if someone says that they get distracted while watching a movie, binge-watching shows, or playing video games. You will get distracted only when you're doing your actual work.

The feeling of satisfaction and thrill that you get while watching a Netflix series right before your exams is incomparable to the time when you are completely free and want to watch it for leisure. Why? Your brain is so stressed that it takes whatever issue is available to escape from reality even if for a few moments. That is why even staring at walls becomes more interesting than actually reading your book. You will suddenly remember to clean your room, do your laundry, clean the dishes, and shop some essentials right before sitting down to do work. Remember, the first leg of resistance is the greatest in terms of power.

Another factor that comes into play is that you tend to get more distracted when working for others.   Like tasks, assignments, or projects that your supervisors give you. We get distracted because we don't directly connect with that work. We don't see the same vision or objective that our supervisors do. We treat it as something we have to get rid of quickly to be free and paradoxically tend to procrastinate more while doing it.

Perhaps, most of you would agree that the biggest source of distraction will be your phone. There's only one solution to cure your distraction from your phone. Shut it down and lock it in your wardrobe. Make it vanish, hide it somewhere your eyes won't find. Your hands only go for it when they find it lying casually and then you subconsciously reach for it. You subconsciously start opening your social media and then you subconsciously start scrolling through the feed.

Wake up! Shut the phone down and be strict with yourself.

If your phone is necessary for you while studying, just uninstall the apps that are distracting you the most. If you find that music distracts you while studying, consider setting a timer for it or limiting listening to it only during breaks. Analyse, adapt, and improve your work ethic.

Distractions can never be removed completely. They will always be there in some miniature form. So do not waste time in devising methods to eradicate all distractions from your life. You might end up dead. Now, it is your choice whether you want them to be conscious or not. By conscious distractions, I am referring to breaks—breaks that you plan and not the ones that you take when you feel like taking one. Breaks which you take from your free will, premeditated, and not from the fatigue of working long hours. They are timed and ritualistic, thus keeping you in momentum while helping to alleviate some fatigue.

Learn the art of taking breaks. At first, you will be inaccurate, you might take a break of a slightly longer duration and another not long enough to remove your stress. But keep tweaking it and you will achieve a steady state of perfect focus which will be highlighted in the next chapter.

Another subtle phenomenon that lurks in our subconsciousness is **entropy**—the gradual decline and fall of all things.

Staying in high inertia for too long is hazardous. You slowly start losing your skills, your charm, and your bonds of friendship.

This process of de-learning will ultimately put you out of practice when you have to start learning anew.

Entropy also sets in when you stop upgrading yourself with the advancements of age. If you are stubborn and stick to the old conventional methods while the world keeps updating itself, then you slowly start going out of fashion.

You definitely must have heard the name of Kodak when you were growing up. But now, you rarely hear its name. Surprisingly, it was the first camera company to launch the first digital camera. However, due to internal feuds that debated the use of digital cameras versus the sale of camera film rolls, the company didn't adapt itself to keep making advanced digital cameras and thus fell out of grace.

Another thing that affects entropy is affluence or superfluity. The more resources you have, the more chaotic you tend to be, and the less streamlined you will become.

A simple example is your smartphone which is loaded with so many apps! There is so much more than necessary for its basic usage, making it sophisticated. You have a social media account, so you have to keep posting or sharing stories to keep it active. You have a credit card, so you don't think twice before buying something unnecessary and will be worried by the month's end to pay its bill. You have a Netflix subscription, so you have to watch the latest show to brag to your friends about.

Imagine, if you had none of this, where would your attention be diverted to? Would you even have any excuse left in your arsenal for not doing work? And would your mind ever drift elsewhere while performing your duty? Since you will have nothing else left to do and no other thing to spend your free time on, you will just focus on doing your work properly and preparing yourself to do it even better the next day. Proper rest, proper sleep, proper diet, and proper planning are the constant forces that help you preserve your momentum.

However, please note that this strategy is only viable when you are trying to prepare for a competitive exam. In the long run, nothing awaits you except for being burnt out of fatigue. Just pick up the momentum with this and use the inertia of motion to rush through your goals like a trailblazer.

Chapter 9

The Zone

There is a gift that lies in waiting for everyone who just perseveres the harsh demotivation of resistance.

It is a very subtle ability that is unlocked for a few moments but it is transient.

This transient space, where you feel like you're indestructible, unbeatable, all-pervasive, and all-knowing is called **The Zone**. It is the highest momentum at which you feel like an omniscient being.

You must have felt it at least once in your life. And you yearn for it. It might also be one of your excuses that you don't feel like studying because you cannot enter this 'zone' that you have once experienced. And though you might have encountered it in one session, you might not encounter it in the next session immediately. It is like a wanton state that comes and goes anytime it pleases. But in reality, it is not so. It will subtly increase in duration if you dedicate more time towards your practice sessions, work, or brainstorming.

What does this 'zone' give you? It is a steady state where you feel immune to the effects of fatigue, you are not troubled by any number of distractions, and you get a subtle 'high' while doing your work. You derive pleasure from working. And the more you work, the prouder you feel about yourself. The effects of dopamine start finally working the way they are supposed to work. They are released in response to the quality and quantity of your work and ensure increased chances of your survival in this cruel world.

The zone doesn't give you any newfound powers. It does not 'increase' your focus or concentration neither does it make you a genius. It just makes you realise your latent powers which you had abandoned in this era of fast information processing, short attention span, and instant gratification.

Let's be honest here. In your childhood, you must have experienced this fleeting feeling while pursuing a favourite hobby like painting a picture to show it to your class teacher, rehearsing a dance move for the seventh time, trying to perfectly sync with the beat, composing a tune with your piano or guitar. The feeling where you shut down all external stimuli.

Sometimes, we miss how attentive and focused we were in our childhood. In the present day, our whole bodies start to itch whenever we sit in the same place doing something for more than ten minutes. Our mind automatically starts to zone out and we start looking for distractions. Our brains cannot handle this monotony, it needs something dynamic to keep happening in front of us. We crave drama and loathe steadiness in our lives.

In reality, no matter how perfect you become, zoning out is inevitable. When you have got rid of the last distraction bothering you, your mind will just decide to zone out instead of focusing on the actual work. But the mistake that we make is that we instantly obey our mind's desire to get a distraction. You should instead take a break and introspect. Do not allow yourself to wilfully be distracted. Introspect that even if your mind is not complying with your set routine, and your set goals, you have covered a certain distance. A distance that you might not have covered at all if you kept engaging with your distractions.

So, no matter how slow it may be, just keep pushing yourself to complete your allotted goals.

For all the other purposes, be as much distracted as you want to be. But to do the work that is needed, the work that you love, you are going to have to wait around for some time.

To enter the zone, just practice sitting for long hours doing the work that you want to do. The first few minutes will be easy. After that, as time passes by, there will be this increasing urge to just shut off everything and leave. And this is where your test will begin. It is the culmination of years and years of discipline and preserved momentum. The longer you stay focused, the longer your zone will be.

You won't realise when you have entered the zone. It will be very subtle. But all of a sudden, you will just realise that all of the urge to quit is gone, and you can sit for an indefinite period of time. This is when you've entered the zone.

What you must know is that entering the zone is not the end; it is just a means. You will get a feeling of invincibility. You will feel that you can conquer the world soon. You will start understanding the intricate details of your work and you might finally start loving your subject.

The Bitter Truth and the Elastic Potential

You now know the secret of the zone. You feel that finally, you can reach your goal. You can finally break that invisible barrier that is keeping you from reaching your dreams. After such a long period, you finally start to believe in your capabilities.

But once again, you hit failure.

After so much hard work, after spending so much time on research and practice, you start questioning yourself about your capacity and wonder whether everything is predestined. You start wondering about hard work, work ethic, the wisdom passed on to you by your elders, and the books that you have read. You start questioning everything. You even start questioning if you are cut out to make it in this world or not. Whether you even deserve to be happy or are you made to just be a failure in life. Such questions will come to you in moments like these which might even take you close to ending your life.

This will happen to you at one point or another. Failure is inevitable for there are many shades of failure—passing the screening test but not getting the desired rank or underscoring rather than failing, given that you were a genius who always got through in the first attempt itself and this was your first failure. Or it might even be plain failure which could have been the result of overestimating yourself or sometimes it is pure bad luck.

This serves as the breakpoint—the actual screening test of nature. Only a chosen few will decide to continue forward on this path once again while the vast majority gives up. Truly, who can bear such courage and hope to try once again the same thing even after doing everything that you could possibly think of? Only madmen and idiots. But only such madmen and idiots can do tasks that the common folk dismiss with logic and reasoning. Only these madmen and idiots hold the potential to become true pioneers and geniuses. I shall call this ability to bounce back to action even after repeated failures as ***Elastic Potential***.

People vary with their elastic potential just as they vary with their inertia. To change your elastic potential, you have to subject yourself to multiple failures and keep coming back to begin right from the start each time you fail. It is a matter of grit and determination. Having a high elastic potential does not guarantee you success but it does increase your chances of getting it.

In the end, let us consider an analogy where you have been designing a rocket trying to escape an inhospitable alien planet.

In the beginning, you weren't even able to start the rocket. But right now, your rocket didn't only launch off beautifully, it was just short of reaching the escape velocity required to escape the planet. From nothing but junk to almost clearing the escape velocity, wouldn't you admit that you have come too far? Now replace the alien planet, the rocket, and the escape velocity with events from your own story, and then pat yourself on the back for having survived so well till now.

For others, you were just a failure. But only you know how close you've come. Do you really plan to quit now and stay stuck on this deserted planet forever?

Have faith in yourself. There's no one else who knows your power and potential better than you. It will take time for the faith and confidence to return but it will return for sure. Start afresh, slow, and steady. Maybe the failure was necessary to give a piece of wisdom that wouldn't have come to you in any other way. Take it with gratitude and start working again. Show the world your true mettle, the material which you are made of, which no one else will have till the end of eternity.

The inertia might be big but once you start moving and working again, it will only get easier to move. For now, you know which paths you have to take and what to avoid. You are wiser than your past self. And so you will reach the momentum much faster than ever before.

Do not be afraid to fall, but be afraid to never be able to rise back up again after falling.

Vectors

Life cannot be only about you and your work, right? There are so many other things that will influence you and your work.

The people around you, the kind of relationships you have with those people, the events and functions that are going to happen—they all will influence your state of inertia.

Vectors, in simplest terms, are directions assigned to any entity. It has two components: a magnitude and a direction.

The objective of our life is to reach our designated goal in the shortest possible amount of time. And to do that we need to have all the external and internal forces acting upon us to align in the same direction. Sadly, that will never be the case.

At any given point, if you analyse, various situations and phenomena draw your attention. Some are urgent and important—they have the greatest magnitude. While the others have decreasing order of importance and magnitude—they may or may not align with your overarching goal.

Here is an example to illustrate what I'm trying to say. Let's suppose you are in a profession that requires you to wear a uniform. It is dirty and you need to clean it before the next day. The second set of uniforms that you had is also dirty. But you also have to finish a PowerPoint presentation that needs to be presented before a board of senior officials the same day. What will you choose? Both are urgent and important tasks but are aligned in two different directions.

Similarly, your commitments with your friends and colleagues, and unexpected plans popping up out of nowhere are vectors. But they aren't always opposing you in your line of work. Learning a new skill that will help you in your work in the future might be in a direction slightly deviated from your line of current work but it is propelling you overall in the forward direction. The good relationships that you have with your seniors, colleagues, friends, and family will keep pushing you ahead adding that extra momentum even if their directions are away from your work. You can even categorise your distractions this way the ones which are propelling you towards your goal and the ones which are keeping you away.

A small piece of advice for relationships: Even if they are not even remotely related to our work, they influence our general state of mind which is responsible for the quality of work that we do. Make sure whatever relationships you have, are positively contributing to your life rather than negatively affecting it. When you are down and surrounded by criticism and failure, your relationship should be the one that lifts you rather than making you question your existence. Do not suffer toxicity when you need to achieve something for yourself and for your family.

Frequency and Resonance

This chapter is for the relationships that you have with your friends and work colleagues.

You will find people whom you start instantly vibing with, with whom your thoughts and ideals will match, you will share the same sense of humour, you will automatically start caring about them, and will start hanging out with them more often. You will become fast friends in no time.

On the other hand, there will be people who despite not having done anything directly to you, will create such an environment that you just can't stand their presence. No fault of theirs but their existence. I am sure you have names popping up in your mind after reading this so I won't take the pain of describing these species anymore.

Let us assume that all of us inherently have a frequency within ourselves. We have a frequency that is unique to us and stays in a plane of existence. The people you vibe with have similar levels of frequency as you and that's why you love to spend more time with them. I would like to call this as finding your **resonance**. The people who do not share the same frequency as you or more specifically who have a frequency lower than you will dampen you out and make you miserable.

We are attracted to people with slightly higher frequency than ours and desist those who have a frequency lower than ours. We tolerate people who have a frequency around our level. If you meet someone with a much higher frequency than yours, you start idolising them. You would like to follow them and even be ready to give up your life for them. But sometimes, you might even feel that you aren't worth getting close to them and reject yourself outright.

Thus, at work, associate yourself with people having higher frequency and do not tolerate people with lower frequency. Strictly for work purposes, higher frequency people will be those with extremely high momentum, who get things done, are helpful, and can teach you new skills. Lower-frequency people are those who drag you down, borrow money from you, take you out to drink and party unnecessarily, and plainly waste your time. The more time you spend with someone, the more your frequency aligns with them.

Make sure that your resonance is with the people of the right frequency so you do not falter in your life.

Elasticity and Plasticity

The cardinal sign of a living being is change.

Every moment we keep changing. The cells in our body grow and die, making us age every second. The compass of our dynamism points to our organic growth.

Our lives are also dynamic as every moment is uncertain. There are highs and lows, growth and decay, new friendships, and heartbreaks. But we keep moving forward.

In Robert Frost's popular poem, *Stopping by the Woods on a Snowy Evening*, the traveller finds a beautiful forest and stops to admire it. But he remembers his duty that he has certain promises to keep and thus ventures ahead.

We all will certainly face this situation in our lives if we haven't already. This beautiful forest will come. It will be enchanting and our minds will never have enough of it. We just wouldn't want to come out of it. This forest could be a period of our lives, like our college days, a failed relationship, or an unrealised dream. We get engrossed in it so much that we might grow old but we don't grow out of it. We get stuck in the same time period, with the same person, and with the same dream.

We refuse to accept the change that comes into our lives and thus suffer for the remainder of it.

In Physics, there are terms called Elasticity and Plasticity. An object is called **elastic** if even after suffering a lot of stress, the object retains its original shape. And if the object is deformed and cannot regain its original shape ever again, it is termed **plastic**. Metals and rubber are examples of elastic objects. Clay is a plastic object.

Ideally, I would advise everyone to be elastic, so that no matter how much stress you undergo, you will always stay the same. You will never lose your integrity. But that is wrong. Sometimes, changing the way you are and the way you work is beneficial in the manner that you will take less stress in the future.

People go through a lot of stress in their lives. More remarkably, they undergo so much stress to attain a single goal. That might be a position, a person, or an object of desire. They have a fear lodged in their minds that if they lose this goal or object, they will be worthless forever. For that one thing, they refuse to undergo any kind of change in their lives. They get stuck in that same place. In that, they begin to stagnate and rot. Their lives turn meaningless; their hopes and dreams slowly start dying away.

It is easier said than done. But with time, we all either get stronger or weaker. In truth, we just get more numb with each passing incident. Some call it maturity but it is really the lack of emotions. The brain just isn't excited anymore with any kind of incident happening. As a result, we become emotionless. Yet there will be moments of life in between when even in this state, we will experience short bursts of true happiness.

Hence, do not try to be either too elastic or too plastic, be yourself and try to accept yourself as you are. Accept what has already happened and make sure that your subsequent decisions are wiser.

The Arrival of Your Final Self

This chapter is only for those who harbour the courage to resist multiple failures. Failure doesn't scare them anymore. They have come to realise their power within for which external events bear little or no effect upon them. Temporary setbacks mean nothing to them. Even after everything is lost, they'll pick themselves up, start from scratch, and build an empire once again.

If you are not one like the above but desire success as eagerly as they do, prepare your mind for a road full of hardships, sweat, toiling, and sacrifices.

Understand, that you are going to have to let go of your present comfortable lifestyle and accept penance. God doesn't want you to win the easy way, so buckle up. You are not one of the chosen ones who get everything handed over to them once they enter the playing field.

You have to earn everything through sheer hard work and penance. But be proud of it—not many can survive this hardship and most end up quitting. Rejoice in the hard moments and celebrate your hard work for these are really the fruits of your hard-earned labour. And lastly, be proud of the person you have become even if the entire world is busy ridiculing you.

Winning is a habit. A habit which is borne from the fruit of countless failures. The guy who you see today constantly winning has suffered so many setbacks in silence that you can hardly keep track of it. Or that person is observant, smart, and learns more from others' mistakes than his own.

Before I conclude, here is a crucial point: Rise and set sail on your mission. Do your work. Nothing will be achieved by theorising your success. The perfect routine can never be made. The perfect mentor can never be found. You only have your mind and your body with you. Use them. Plan but don't idolise. Make mistakes and learn to modify your approach.

Keep adapting to your circumstances and never give up till you attain your final self.